Welcome to "Unveiling the Spectrum: Triumphs and Trials of LGBTQ Lives." In these pages, we embark on a journey of understanding, compassion, and celebration as we explore the diverse range of experiences within the LGBTQ community. This book is a testament to the remarkable individuals who have faced tremendous triumphs and formidable trials while navigating the complexities of their identities.

Within these chapters, we delve into the various dimensions of LGBTQ lives, shedding light on the triumphs and challenges encountered by individuals who identify as lesbian, gay, bisexual, transgender, queer, or any other sexual orientation or gender identity along the vast spectrum. By exploring their stories, we hope to foster empathy, understanding, and respect for the rich tapestry of LGBTQ experiences.

In Chapter 1, "Unveiling the Spectrum: Understanding LGBTQ Identities," we lay the foundation for our exploration. We delve into the different sexual orientations and gender identities within the LGBTQ community, providing insights into the challenges of societal norms, self-acceptance, and the complex journey of coming to terms with one's identity.

Chapter 2, "Personal Triumphs: Stories of Overcoming Adversity," introduces us to inspiring narratives of LGBTQ individuals who have triumphed over adversity. Through their stories, we witness the resilience, strength, and success found in various aspects of their lives, such as relationships, careers, activism, and personal growth.

However, the journey of LGBTQ lives is not without its trials. In Chapter 3, "Trials and Challenges: Confronting Adversity," we explore the obstacles faced by LGBTQ individuals. We address the discrimination, prejudice, and societal barriers that persist, while also examining the impact on mental health, familial and societal acceptance, and the ongoing struggle against systemic oppression.

Chapter 4, "Intersectionality and Diversity: Celebrating Unique Journeys," invites us to embrace the diversity within the LGBTQ community. We delve into the intersectional experiences of individuals, examining how their race, ethnicity, religion, and ability intersect with their LGBTQ identities, presenting both the challenges and triumphs that arise from these intersections.

Support and allyship play pivotal roles in the LGBTQ community, which we explore in Chapter 5, "Allies and Support: Building Inclusive Communities." We examine the significance of allies, the vital role of support networks, safe spaces, and the contributions of advocacy organizations in creating inclusive environments.

While progress has been made in LGBTQ rights and acceptance, there is still much work to be done. In Chapter 6, "Striving for Equality: Progress and Ongoing Challenges," we reflect on historical milestones, ongoing battles for equality, and the importance of education and awareness in fostering a more inclusive society.

As we conclude this journey together, we invite you to reflect on the stories shared and the insights gained. "Unveiling the Spectrum: Triumphs and Trials of LGBTQ Lives" serves as a reminder that behind each triumph and trial lies a human experience that deserves to be understood, respected, and celebrated. May these pages inspire empathy, compassion, and an unwavering commitment to fostering a world where every individual is valued for their authentic selves.

Join us now as we embark on this enlightening exploration of triumphs, trials, and the beautiful spectrum of LGBTQ lives.

TABLE OF CONTENTS

Introduction

- Education and Awareness for a More Inclusive Society

Conclusion: Journeying Forward with Resilience and Hope

CHAPTER ONE

UNVEILING THE SPECTRUM:

UNDERSTANDING LGBTQ IDENTITIES

Exploring Sexual Orientations

Introduction:

In this chapter, we embark on a comprehensive exploration of the diverse range of sexual orientations within the LGBTQ community. By delving into the intricacies of sexual orientation, we aim to provide a deeper understanding of the experiences, challenges, and triumphs that individuals across the spectrum encounter in their lives. Join us as we navigate through the rich tapestry of sexual orientations, fostering empathy, awareness, and acceptance.

1. Defining Sexual Orientation:

Sexual orientation is a fundamental aspect of human identity that encompasses an individual's enduring pattern of emotional, romantic, and/or sexual attractions. It is an integral part of who we are and should be recognized and respected as such. Understanding the intricacies of sexual orientation lays the groundwork for

appreciating the diversity within the LGBTQ
community.

2. Common Sexual Orientations:

Within the LGBTQ community, several sexual
orientations are widely recognized and
experienced by individuals worldwide.
Homosexuality, characterized by same-gender
attractions, has been a focal point of LGBTQ
activism and acceptance. Heterosexuality, the
attraction to individuals of a different gender, is
the dominant sexual orientation in society.
Bisexuality, the attraction to both same and
different genders, presents its own unique
experiences and challenges. By exploring these
common sexual orientations, we gain insight
into the complexities and dynamics of diverse
attractions.

3. Fluid Sexual Orientations:

Sexual orientation is not always fixed and
immutable. Many individuals experience fluidity
in their attractions, where their preferences
may change or evolve over time. This fluidity
may manifest as shifts in the gender(s)
individuals are attracted to or varying degrees

of attraction. Recognizing and accepting the fluidity within sexual orientations is crucial in embracing the diversity of human experiences and identities.

4. Less Common Sexual Orientations:

Beyond the more commonly known sexual orientations, there exist a multitude of less recognized or understood orientations within the LGBTQ community. Pansexuality refers to the attraction to individuals regardless of their gender, encompassing a broad spectrum of identities. Asexuality, on the other hand, describes individuals who experience little to no sexual attraction, often forming deep emotional connections instead. Demisexuality represents individuals who experience sexual attraction only after developing a strong emotional bond. Exploring these less common sexual orientations allows us to broaden our understanding of human diversity and challenge societal norms.

5. Coming Out:

Coming out is a significant milestone in the lives of many LGBTQ individuals. It involves disclosing one's sexual orientation to others, often with the aim of living authentically and openly. The coming-out process varies greatly from person to person, encompassing a range of emotions, fears, and potential consequences. Understanding the significance of coming out and the support needed during this vulnerable period is essential for fostering inclusivity and creating safe spaces for LGBTQ individuals.

6. Intersectionality and Sexual Orientation:

Sexual orientation does not exist in isolation; it intersects with other aspects of identity, such as race, ethnicity, culture, religion, and socioeconomic status. These intersecting identities shape the experiences and challenges faced by LGBTQ individuals. Acknowledging the unique intersectionalities within sexual orientation allows us to grasp the complexities of individuals' lives and work towards dismantling the multiple forms of discrimination and oppression they may encounter.

7. Challenges and Triumphs:

Individuals with diverse sexual orientations face a range of challenges, including discrimination, prejudice, and the internal struggle for self-acceptance. Homophobia, biphobia, and heteronormativity are pervasive societal forces that perpetuate stigma and marginalization. However, within these challenges lie triumphs of self-discovery, resilience, and personal growth. By sharing stories of those who have embraced their sexual orientations with pride and authenticity, we celebrate the courage and strength of individuals who have overcome societal barriers.

As we conclude this chapter of exploration into sexual orientations, it is evident that the understanding and acceptance of diverse attractions are pivotal in building an inclusive society. The multifaceted nature of sexual orientation extends beyond the conventional labels and embraces the richness of human experiences.

By embracing the intricacies of sexual orientation, we acknowledge that it exists on a continuum, allowing room for individuals to express their unique attractions and desires. This recognition fosters a more nuanced understanding of human sexuality and challenges the binary notions that have long constrained our understanding of love and relationships.

Furthermore, recognizing the fluidity within sexual orientations is essential in promoting inclusivity and validating individuals' evolving experiences. The fluidity concept acknowledges that attractions and desires can evolve and change, freeing individuals from rigid expectations and allowing them to embrace their authentic selves without fear or judgment.

While common sexual orientations such as homosexuality, heterosexuality, and bisexuality have gained greater visibility and acceptance, it is crucial to shed light on the less commonly known orientations. Pansexuality, with its emphasis on love and attraction regardless of gender, challenges the boundaries that limit our understanding of relationships. Asexuality highlights the diverse ways in which individuals experience and express intimacy, emphasizing emotional connections over sexual desire. Demisexuality, often misunderstood or overlooked, underscores the importance of emotional connection as a precursor to sexual attraction.

The journey of self-discovery and acceptance for individuals with diverse sexual orientations often involves the courageous act of coming out. Coming out is a deeply personal and transformative process that varies greatly from person to person. It involves confronting fears, navigating societal expectations, and seeking support from trusted individuals or communities. Creating an environment of acceptance and understanding is crucial in easing the coming-out process and ensuring that LGBTQ individuals can live their lives authentically and with pride.

An intersectional approach to understanding sexual orientation recognizes that it intertwines with other facets of identity. Race, ethnicity, religion, and socioeconomic status intersect with sexual orientation, shaping individuals' experiences and vulnerabilities. Recognizing and addressing these intersectional challenges is essential in creating an inclusive and equitable society that uplifts and supports all LGBTQ individuals.

While the journey of individuals with diverse sexual orientations is marked by challenges, it is equally important to highlight their triumphs. From advocacy and activism to personal growth and self-acceptance, LGBTQ individuals have showcased immense resilience, courage, and determination. Their stories of triumph inspire others to embrace their identities, challenge societal norms, and strive for a more inclusive future.

In conclusion, exploring sexual orientations requires an open mind, empathy, and a willingness to challenge preconceived notions. By delving into the complexities of sexual orientation, we can foster greater understanding, acceptance, and celebration of the diverse range of attractions that exist within the LGBTQ community. As we continue on this journey of discovery, let us embrace the spectrum of sexual orientations, recognizing the triumphs, honoring the challenges, and advocating for a world where every individual is free to love and be loved authentically.

Navigating Gender Identities

In this chapter, we delve into the fascinating
and diverse landscape of gender identities
within the LGBTQ community. Gender identity
is an essential aspect of selfhood that goes
beyond the binary notions of male and female.
By exploring the intricacies of gender identities,
we aim to foster understanding, respect, and
inclusivity for individuals who identify beyond
the traditional gender norms. Join us as we
navigate the rich tapestry of gender identities,
embracing the triumphs and trials faced by
those who dare to live authentically.

1. Understanding Gender Identity:

- Define gender identity as an individual's deeply felt sense of being male, female, or something else.

- Explore the concept of gender as a social construct and how it differs from biological sex.

2. Binary and Non-Binary Gender Identities:

- Examine the traditional binary understanding of gender as male or female.

- Introduce non-binary identities, which encompass a wide range of gender expressions outside the binary spectrum.

- Discuss the experiences and challenges faced by individuals who identify as non-binary.

3. Transgender Identities:

- Provide an overview of transgender identities, where individuals' gender identity does not align with the sex assigned at birth.

- Explore the diverse experiences and journeys of transgender individuals, including social transition, medical transition, and the importance of gender-affirming support.

4. Gender Dysphoria and Resilience:

- Discuss gender dysphoria, a condition experienced by some transgender individuals, characterized by distress due to the incongruence between their gender identity and assigned sex.

- Highlight the resilience and strength demonstrated by transgender individuals in navigating gender dysphoria and pursuing a path of self-discovery and authenticity.

5. Gender Expression and Presentation:

- Explore the ways in which individuals express their gender identities through clothing, hairstyles, mannerisms, and other external expressions.

- Discuss the significance of gender expression in affirming one's identity and the societal challenges and triumphs associated with gender presentation.

6. Intersectionality and Gender Identity:

- Examine how gender identity intersects with other aspects of identity, such as race, ethnicity, and socioeconomic status.

- Discuss the unique experiences and challenges faced by individuals with intersecting gender and cultural identities.

7. Challenges and Triumphs:

- Address the challenges faced by individuals with diverse gender identities, including discrimination, lack of legal recognition, and limited access to healthcare.

- Share stories of triumph and resilience, highlighting the achievements, advocacy, and community support that contribute to positive change and acceptance.

Conclusion:

As we conclude this chapter, it is evident that gender identities extend far beyond the binary framework. Navigating the intricacies of gender is a deeply personal and transformative journey for individuals who identify outside traditional norms. By embracing and celebrating the diverse range of gender identities, we can foster a more inclusive and understanding society. Let us honor the triumphs, acknowledge the trials, and work towards creating a world where individuals of all gender identities are embraced, respected, and empowered to live their lives authentically.

Challenges Of Societal Norms And Self - Acceptance

In this chapter, we delve into the complex dynamics between societal norms and the journey of self-acceptance within the LGBTQ community. Society's expectations and cultural norms often pose significant challenges for individuals who deviate from heteronormative and cisgender norms. By exploring these challenges and the transformative process of self-acceptance, we aim to shed light on the triumphs and trials faced by LGBTQ individuals as they navigate their identities and strive for authenticity.

1. Heteronormativity and Cisnormativity:

- Define heteronormativity as the societal assumption that heterosexuality is the norm and cisnormativity as the assumption that being cisgender is the norm.

- Explore the ways in which these norms impact LGBTQ individuals, perpetuating stereotypes, discrimination, and marginalization.

2. Coming to Terms with Identity:

- Discuss the personal journey of self-discovery and self-acceptance that LGBTQ individuals undertake.

- Highlight the internal struggles, confusion, and fear that individuals often experience as they come to terms with their identities.

3. Cultural and Religious Challenges:

- Examine the challenges faced by LGBTQ individuals within various cultural and religious contexts.

- Discuss the conflict between personal identity and cultural or religious expectations, and the impact on self-acceptance.

4. Family and Social Rejection:

- Address the difficulties LGBTQ individuals may encounter in coming out to their families and social circles.

- Explore the potential for rejection, strained relationships, and the emotional toll it can have on individuals' well-being.

5. Bullying, Discrimination, and Violence:

- Shed light on the prevalence of bullying, discrimination, and violence directed towards LGBTQ individuals.

- Discuss the detrimental effects on mental health, self-esteem, and overall quality of life, and the importance of creating safe and inclusive spaces.

6. Intersectionality and Multiple Forms of Oppression:

- Explore how LGBTQ individuals may face multiple forms of oppression due to intersecting identities, such as race, ethnicity, disability, or socioeconomic status.

- Discuss the unique challenges faced by individuals who navigate the intersectionality of their identities and the need for intersectional approaches to advocacy and support.

7. Self-Acceptance and Resilience:

- Highlight the transformative process of self-acceptance and the importance of self-love and self-care.

- Share stories of resilience, personal growth, and triumph, demonstrating the strength and courage of LGBTQ individuals in embracing their authentic selves.

Conclusion:

As we conclude this chapter, it is evident that societal norms and the journey of self-acceptance pose significant challenges for LGBTQ individuals. The pressure to conform to heteronormative and cisnormative standards, combined with cultural and religious expectations, can create internal turmoil and external barriers. However, the stories of triumph and resilience showcase the power of self-acceptance and the ability to transcend societal constraints. By challenging and dismantling oppressive norms, fostering inclusivity, and creating supportive communities, we can work towards a society where all individuals, regardless of their sexual orientation or gender identity, can thrive and live authentically.

CHAPTER TWO

PERSONAL TRIUMPHS

Relationships And Love

Love knows no boundaries, and individuals across the spectrum of sexual orientations and gender identities experience deep connections, intimacy, and affection. By exploring the diverse aspects of LGBTQ relationships, we aim to foster understanding, respect, and acceptance for all forms of love. Join us as we navigate the joys, challenges, and triumphs of relationships and love within the LGBTQ community.

1. Relationship Dynamics:

- Explore the various dynamics and structures of LGBTQ relationships, including same-sex relationships, different-gender relationships, and non-monogamous relationships.

- Discuss the unique strengths and challenges that arise within LGBTQ relationships, emphasizing the importance of communication, trust, and mutual respect.

2. Building Healthy Relationships:

- Highlight the essential elements of building healthy and fulfilling relationships, including effective communication, emotional support, and shared values.

- Address the challenges faced by LGBTQ individuals in establishing and maintaining healthy relationships within societal and cultural contexts.

3. Dating and Intimacy:

- Discuss the experiences and challenges of LGBTQ individuals in the realm of dating and finding compatible partners.

- Explore the importance of consent, boundaries, and sexual health within LGBTQ relationships, emphasizing the need for inclusive and comprehensive education.

4. Family and Parenting:

- Address the unique experiences of LGBTQ individuals in forming families, including

adoption, surrogacy, and co-parenting
arrangements.

- Discuss the legal, societal, and emotional
challenges faced by LGBTQ parents and their
children, as well as the triumphs of creating
loving and supportive family units.

5. Long-Term Commitment:

- Explore the experiences of LGBTQ individuals
in long-term committed relationships, including
marriage, civil partnerships, and commitment
ceremonies.

- Discuss the significance of legal recognition
and equality in fostering stable and secure
relationships within the LGBTQ community.

6. Intersectionality in Relationships:

- Examine how intersectional identities, such
as race, ethnicity, and socioeconomic status,
intersect with relationships within the LGBTQ
community.

- Address the unique challenges faced by
LGBTQ individuals with intersecting identities

and the importance of inclusivity and cultural competency in relationships.

7. Love and Resilience:

- Share stories of love, resilience, and triumph within LGBTQ relationships, highlighting the strength and commitment of individuals who navigate the complexities of societal norms and prejudices.

- Discuss the importance of celebrating and honoring LGBTQ love stories, contributing to greater acceptance and understanding.

It is evident that relationships and love within the LGBTQ community are rich, diverse, and profound. LGBTQ individuals form deep connections, create families, and experience the joys and challenges of love just like any other individual. By embracing and celebrating the spectrum of relationships, we can foster a more inclusive and loving society. Let us honor the triumphs, navigate the challenges, and work towards a world where all forms of love are recognized, respected, and celebrated without discrimination.

Carrier Success and Entrepreneurship

Despite the challenges faced, LGBTQ
individuals have made significant contributions

to various industries, professions, and entrepreneurial endeavors. By delving into the triumphs and trials of career pursuits, we aim to inspire and empower LGBTQ individuals to thrive professionally and create their own paths of success.

1. Workplace Diversity and Inclusion:

- Discuss the importance of workplace diversity and inclusion for LGBTQ individuals.

- Address the progress made in creating inclusive work environments, as well as the existing challenges and the need for continued advocacy.

2. Overcoming Workplace Discrimination:

- Highlight the discrimination and biases that LGBTQ individuals may face in the workplace.

- Explore strategies for overcoming workplace discrimination and creating safe and supportive professional spaces.

3. LGBTQ Professionals and Role Models:

- Showcase the achievements and contributions of successful LGBTQ professionals across various industries.

- Discuss the significance of LGBTQ role models in inspiring and mentoring aspiring professionals.

4. Entrepreneurship and Business Ownership:

- Explore the experiences and successes of LGBTQ entrepreneurs who have started their own businesses.

- Discuss the unique challenges and opportunities faced by LGBTQ entrepreneurs and the importance of creating inclusive business environments.

5. Building Professional Networks:

- Address the significance of professional networks and support systems for LGBTQ individuals.

- Discuss the benefits of networking, mentorship, and community engagement in fostering career growth and success.

6. Balancing Identity and Professionalism:

- Discuss the challenges of navigating one's LGBTQ identity in professional settings.

- Explore strategies for maintaining authenticity while balancing professionalism and career advancement.

7. Embracing Leadership and Breaking Glass Ceilings:

- Highlight the achievements of LGBTQ leaders and trailblazers who have shattered barriers and made significant impacts in their fields.

- Discuss the importance of LGBTQ individuals embracing leadership roles and advocating for equal opportunities within their professions.

8. Mental Health and Career Success:

- Address the impact of societal pressures, discrimination, and stigma on the mental health of LGBTQ professionals.

- Discuss the importance of self-care, seeking support, and fostering resilience for maintaining career success.

It is evident that LGBTQ individuals have made remarkable strides in achieving career success and making significant contributions to various industries. Despite the challenges faced, the triumphs of LGBTQ professionals and entrepreneurs serve as inspirations for others to pursue their career aspirations without compromising their identities. By fostering inclusive workplaces, promoting diversity, and empowering LGBTQ individuals to thrive professionally, we can create a future where career success knows no boundaries. Let us celebrate the achievements, overcome the trials, and continue to pave the way for a more inclusive and equitable professional landscape for all.

Activism And Making A Difference

We explore the power of activism within the LGBTQ community and the significant impact it has had on advancing rights, equality, and acceptance. Activism plays a vital role in challenging societal norms, advocating for change, and creating a more inclusive and equitable world for LGBTQ individuals. By examining the triumphs and trials of activism, we aim to inspire and empower readers to make a difference in their communities and contribute to the ongoing fight for LGBTQ rights and social justice.

1. Understanding LGBTQ Activism:

- Define LGBTQ activism and its historical significance in the fight for LGBTQ rights.

- Explore the various forms of activism, including grassroots organizing, protests, advocacy, and community building.

2. The Stonewall Uprising and its Legacy:

- Discuss the Stonewall Uprising as a pivotal moment in LGBTQ history and the catalyst for the modern LGBTQ rights movement.

- Explore the lasting impact of Stonewall on activism and its significance in inspiring future generations of activists.

3. Intersectionality and Inclusive Activism:

- Examine the importance of intersectionality in LGBTQ activism, recognizing and addressing the diverse experiences and needs of individuals with intersecting identities.

- Discuss the challenges and triumphs of inclusive activism that embraces diversity and fights for social justice for all marginalized communities.

4. Legislative Advocacy and Policy Change:

- Explore the role of legislative advocacy in advancing LGBTQ rights and protections.

- Highlight key legislative milestones, such as marriage equality, anti-discrimination laws, and healthcare access, and the activists who played significant roles in their achievement.

5. Community Organizing and Grassroots Movements:

- Discuss the power of community organizing and grassroots movements in effecting change at the local level.

- Highlight the importance of building strong community networks, organizing Pride events,

support groups, and safe spaces for LGBTQ
individuals.

6. Digital Activism and Social Media:

- Examine the role of digital activism and
social media platforms in amplifying LGBTQ
voices and promoting awareness.

- Discuss the benefits and challenges of online
activism, including online harassment and the
importance of maintaining safe and inclusive
online spaces.

7. Global LGBTQ Activism:

- Explore LGBTQ activism on a global scale,
recognizing the diverse challenges faced by
LGBTQ individuals in different countries and
cultures.

- Highlight international LGBTQ rights
movements, activists, and the ongoing fight for
global equality.

8. Activism in Everyday Life:

- Discuss ways in which individuals can incorporate activism into their daily lives and make a difference in their immediate communities.

- Provide practical tips for supporting LGBTQ organizations, engaging in allyship, and educating others to foster acceptance and inclusivity.

From historic uprisings to ongoing grassroots efforts, activists have been at the forefront of creating positive change for the LGBTQ community. By embracing activism and making a difference in our own lives, we contribute to a more inclusive and equitable society. Let us celebrate the triumphs of LGBTQ activists, learn from their struggles, and join the ongoing fight for LGBTQ rights and social justice. Together, we can create a world where all individuals, regardless of their sexual orientation or gender identity, can live with dignity, respect, and equality.

Personal Growth And Self Discovery

Coming to terms with one's sexual orientation or gender identity can be a profound and life-changing experience. By delving into the triumphs and trials of personal growth and self-discovery, we aim to inspire readers to embrace their authentic selves, foster self-acceptance, and embark on a path of self-discovery and personal fulfillment.

1. The Journey of Self-Discovery:

- Discuss the personal journey of self-discovery that LGBTQ individuals often experience, including the questioning, exploration, and acceptance of their sexual orientation or gender identity.

- Explore the emotional, psychological, and social aspects of the journey and the importance of self-reflection and self-awareness.

2. Embracing Authenticity:

- Highlight the significance of embracing authenticity and living true to oneself.

- Discuss the challenges faced by LGBTQ individuals in reconciling societal expectations with their authentic identities, and the empowerment that comes with embracing one's true self.

3. Self-Acceptance and Self-Love:

- Explore the process of self-acceptance and self-love for LGBTQ individuals.

- Discuss the importance of self-compassion, self-care, and developing a positive self-image while navigating societal pressures and stereotypes.

4. Building a Supportive Network:

- Address the importance of building a supportive network of friends, family, and community for LGBTQ individuals on their journey of personal growth and self-discovery.

- Discuss the role of support groups, LGBTQ organizations, and online communities in providing guidance, acceptance, and a sense of belonging.

5. Mental Health and Well-Being:

- Address the unique mental health challenges faced by LGBTQ individuals and the importance of prioritizing mental well-being.

- Discuss the importance of seeking professional help, practicing self-care, and developing coping strategies to foster emotional resilience.

6. Exploring Identity and Expression:

- Discuss the exploration and expression of gender identity and sexual orientation within the LGBTQ community.

- Explore the various forms of gender expression and the fluidity and diversity of sexual orientations, emphasizing the freedom to explore and define oneself on an individual basis.

7. Navigating Relationships and Intimacy:

- Address the challenges and triumphs of navigating relationships and intimacy while on the journey of personal growth and self-discovery.

- Discuss the importance of open communication, setting boundaries, and fostering healthy connections with others.

8. Spirituality and Finding Meaning:

- Explore the intersection of spirituality and personal growth for LGBTQ individuals.

- Discuss the diverse experiences and perspectives on spirituality within the LGBTQ community, emphasizing the importance of finding meaning and purpose in one's life.

As we conclude this chapter, it is evident that personal growth and self-discovery are transformative journeys for LGBTQ individuals. By embracing authenticity, fostering self-acceptance, and nurturing personal well-being, individuals can embark on a path of self-discovery and personal fulfillment. The triumphs and trials of personal growth contribute to a greater understanding of oneself, fostering resilience, and creating a strong foundation for living an authentic and fulfilling life. Let us celebrate the beauty of personal growth and self-discovery within the LGBTQ community and support one another on our individual journeys of self-discovery and personal fulfillment.

CHAPTER THREE

TRIALS AND CHALLENGES

Discrimination And Prejudice

We confront the sobering reality of discrimination and prejudice that persistently impact the lives of LGBTQ individuals. Despite the progress made in advancing LGBTQ rights, many individuals still face discrimination, marginalization, and prejudice based on their sexual orientation or gender identity. By shedding light on the triumphs and trials of navigating discrimination and prejudice, we aim to raise awareness, promote empathy, and advocate for a more inclusive and equal society.

1. Understanding Discrimination and Prejudice:

- Define discrimination and prejudice and their impact on the lives of LGBTQ individuals.

- Explore the various forms of discrimination, including legal, institutional, and interpersonal discrimination.

2. Legal and Policy Challenges:

- Discuss the legal challenges faced by LGBTQ individuals, such as the lack of comprehensive anti-discrimination laws and barriers to legal recognition.

- Highlight landmark legal cases and legislative efforts that have shaped LGBTQ rights and protections, as well as ongoing challenges and the need for continued advocacy.

3. Hate Crimes and Violence:

- Address the alarming rates of hate crimes and violence targeting LGBTQ individuals.

- Discuss the impact of hate crimes on the physical and emotional well-being of victims, and the importance of combating hate and promoting safety and justice.

4. Microaggressions and Everyday Prejudice:

- Explore the impact of microaggressions, subtle forms of discrimination, and everyday prejudices on the lives of LGBTQ individuals.

- Discuss strategies for recognizing and addressing microaggressions, fostering allyship, and promoting inclusive language and behaviors.

5. Intersectionality and Multiple Forms of Discrimination:

- Examine the intersectionality of identities and how it compounds the experiences of discrimination and prejudice for LGBTQ individuals with intersecting identities.

- Discuss the importance of recognizing and addressing multiple forms of discrimination, including racism, ableism, and sexism within the LGBTQ community.

6. Mental and Emotional Impact:

- Address the mental and emotional toll of experiencing discrimination and prejudice.

- Discuss the impact on mental health, self-esteem, and overall well-being, as well as the importance of accessible mental health support and resilience-building.

7. Resisting and Overcoming Discrimination:

- Highlight stories of resilience and resistance against discrimination and prejudice within the LGBTQ community.

- Discuss strategies for combating discrimination, promoting equality, and advocating for LGBTQ rights through community organizing, education, and legislative efforts.

8. Building Inclusive Communities:

- Discuss the importance of building inclusive communities that reject discrimination and embrace diversity.

- Explore ways in which individuals, organizations, and communities can create safe and supportive spaces for LGBTQ individuals, fostering acceptance and equality.

By shedding light on these issues, we can foster understanding, empathy, and the collective determination to create a more inclusive and equal society. Let us stand in solidarity against discrimination, advocate for change, and work towards a future where all individuals, regardless of their sexual orientation or gender identity, can live free from discrimination and prejudice. Together, we can build a society that celebrates diversity, respects human rights, and affirms the inherent dignity of every individual.

SOCIETAL BARRIERS AND LEGAL CHALLENGES

Here, we examine the societal barriers and legal challenges that LGBTQ individuals face in their pursuit of equality, acceptance, and full participation in society. Despite advancements in LGBTQ rights, systemic barriers and discriminatory practices continue to hinder progress. By exploring the triumphs and trials of confronting societal barriers and legal challenges, we aim to raise awareness, advocate for change, and promote a more inclusive and equitable society.

1. Stigma and Social Rejection:

- Discuss the pervasive stigma surrounding LGBTQ individuals and the social rejection they often encounter.

- Examine the impact of stigma on mental health, relationships, and overall well-being, emphasizing the need for education and societal change.

2. Family and Relationship Recognition:

- Address the legal challenges faced by LGBTQ individuals in areas such as marriage equality, adoption, and parental rights.

- Explore the triumphs and ongoing struggles for equal recognition of LGBTQ families and relationships.

3. Healthcare Disparities:

- Examine the healthcare disparities experienced by LGBTQ individuals, including barriers to access, discrimination, and inadequate healthcare services.

- Discuss the importance of LGBTQ-inclusive healthcare policies and the efforts to improve healthcare outcomes for the community.

4. Education and Bullying:

- Discuss the challenges faced by LGBTQ students in educational institutions, including bullying, discrimination, and lack of inclusive policies.

- Highlight efforts to promote safe and inclusive schools, provide support for LGBTQ students, and advocate for comprehensive LGBTQ-inclusive education.

5. Employment Discrimination:

- Address the barriers and discrimination faced by LGBTQ individuals in the workplace, including hiring practices, workplace harassment, and lack of employment protections.

- Discuss the legal landscape, ongoing advocacy efforts, and the importance of inclusive workplace policies.

6. Access to Housing and Homelessness:

- Examine the challenges faced by LGBTQ individuals in accessing safe and inclusive housing.

- Address the disproportionate rates of homelessness among LGBTQ youth and the need for LGBTQ-inclusive housing policies and support services.

7. Transgender Rights and Legal Recognition:

- Explore the unique challenges faced by transgender individuals in obtaining legal recognition of their gender identity.

- Discuss issues such as name and gender marker changes, access to healthcare, and the ongoing fight for transgender rights.

8. International Perspectives and Global Challenges:

- Address the global challenges faced by LGBTQ individuals in countries with hostile legal and societal climates.

- Highlight international efforts, organizations, and movements advocating for LGBTQ rights and the need for global solidarity.

As we conclude this part, it is evident that
LGBTQ individuals continue to face societal
barriers and legal challenges that impede their
full participation in society. By understanding
and addressing these issues, we can work
towards dismantling systemic barriers,
advocating for legal protections, and fostering a
more inclusive and equitable society. Let us
stand together in challenging discriminatory
practices, promoting understanding, and
advocating for LGBTQ rights at local, national,
and global levels. Through collective action and
ongoing efforts, we can create a future where
all LGBTQ individuals are treated with dignity,
respect, and equal rights under the law.

MENTAL HEALTH AND WELL-BEING

We delve into the critical topic of mental health and well-being within the LGBTQ community. LGBTQ individuals often face unique challenges that can impact their mental and emotional well-being. By exploring the triumphs and trials of navigating mental health, we aim to promote awareness, provide support, and encourage the development of strategies and resources for positive mental health and well-being.

1. LGBTQ Mental Health: Understanding the Landscape

- Discuss the specific mental health challenges faced by LGBTQ individuals, including higher rates of depression, anxiety, and suicide.

- Examine the impact of societal stigma, discrimination, and internalized homophobia or transphobia on mental well-being.

2. Navigating Coming Out and Self-Acceptance

- Address the psychological journey of coming out and the impact it can have on mental health.

- Explore strategies for self-acceptance, coping with rejection, and fostering a positive sense of identity.

3. Access to LGBTQ-Inclusive Mental Health Care

- Discuss the importance of LGBTQ-inclusive mental health care and the barriers LGBTQ individuals may face in accessing appropriate support.

- Highlight efforts to improve accessibility and advocate for LGBTQ-inclusive mental health services.

4. Building Resilience and Coping Strategies

- Provide practical tips and strategies for building resilience and promoting mental well-being.

- Discuss the importance of self-care, stress management, and healthy coping mechanisms within the LGBTQ community.

5. Intersectionality and Mental Health

- Examine the intersectionality of LGBTQ identities with other marginalized identities and its impact on mental health.

- Address the unique experiences and challenges faced by LGBTQ individuals with intersecting identities, such as race, disability, or socioeconomic status.

6. Supportive Networks and Community Resources

- Highlight the significance of support networks, community resources, and LGBTQ organizations in promoting mental health and well-being.

- Discuss the role of peer support, counseling services, and online communities in providing a sense of belonging and support.

7. Substance Abuse and Addiction

- Address the higher rates of substance abuse and addiction within the LGBTQ community and the underlying factors contributing to this issue.

- Discuss the importance of prevention, early intervention, and access to LGBTQ-inclusive substance abuse treatment programs.

8. Allyship and Mental Health Advocacy

- Explore the role of allies in supporting the mental health and well-being of LGBTQ individuals.

- Discuss how individuals can become effective allies, challenge stigma, and advocate for mental health support and resources.

It is evident that mental health and well-being are crucial aspects of LGBTQ individuals' lives. By understanding the unique challenges they face, promoting awareness, and providing support, we can foster a culture of compassion, acceptance, and mental well-being within the LGBTQ community. Let us work together to break the stigma surrounding mental health, improve access to LGBTQ-inclusive mental health care, and promote resilience and well-being for all LGBTQ individuals. Through our collective efforts, we can create a future where mental health is prioritized, support is readily

available, and all LGBTQ individuals can thrive
and flourish.

FAMILY AND COMMUNITY ACCEPTANCE

In this part of the chapter, we explore the
triumphs and trials of family and community
acceptance within the LGBTQ community.
Acceptance from loved ones and the broader

community plays a vital role in the well-being and overall happiness of LGBTQ individuals. By examining the journey of family and community acceptance, we aim to highlight the importance of understanding, support, and creating inclusive environments that embrace diversity.

1. Coming Out to Family:

- Discuss the process of coming out to family members and the emotional challenges it entails.

- Explore various reactions and responses from families, including acceptance, rejection, and ongoing negotiations of understanding.

2. Navigating Family Dynamics:

- Address the dynamics that LGBTQ individuals may encounter within their families, such as cultural or religious influences and generational gaps.

- Discuss strategies for fostering open communication, empathy, and understanding among family members.

3. Parental Acceptance and Support:

- Highlight the significant role of parental acceptance and support in the well-being of LGBTQ individuals.

- Share stories of parental acceptance and the positive impact it has on the individual's self-esteem and overall happiness.

4. Siblings and Extended Family:

- Explore the role of siblings and extended family members in the journey of acceptance.

- Discuss the potential challenges and opportunities for support and understanding within these relationships.

5. Chosen Family:

- Discuss the concept of chosen family, where LGBTQ individuals find support and acceptance from friends and community outside their biological families.

- Highlight the importance of these relationships and the sense of belonging they provide.

6. Faith Communities and Acceptance:

- Address the intersection of LGBTQ identity and religious or spiritual beliefs.

- Explore the diverse experiences of LGBTQ individuals within faith communities, including acceptance, rejection, and reconciliation.

7. Creating Inclusive Communities:

- Discuss the importance of fostering inclusive and supportive communities for LGBTQ individuals.

- Highlight initiatives, organizations, and resources that promote acceptance and equality within neighborhoods, schools, and workplaces.

8. Advocacy for Family and Community Acceptance:

- Discuss the role of advocacy in promoting family and community acceptance.

- Highlight campaigns, organizations, and initiatives that work towards creating a more accepting and inclusive society.

Conclusion:

As we conclude this chapter, it is clear that family and community acceptance play a crucial role in the lives of LGBTQ individuals. By sharing stories of triumph and resilience, we can inspire understanding, empathy, and positive change within families and communities. Let us work towards creating environments that embrace diversity, where all LGBTQ individuals can find acceptance, support, and love. Through education, dialogue, and advocacy, we can foster a future where family and community acceptance are the norm, allowing LGBTQ individuals to live authentically and thrive within their social networks.

INTERSECTIONALITY AND DIVERSITY

Embracing Multicultural LGBTQ Experiences

In this chapter, we celebrate the diverse and rich experiences of LGBTQ individuals from multicultural backgrounds. LGBTQ identities intersect with various cultural, ethnic, and religious backgrounds, shaping unique experiences and challenges. By exploring the triumphs and trials of multicultural LGBTQ experiences, we aim to foster understanding, promote inclusivity, and celebrate the diversity within the LGBTQ community.

1. Intersectionality and Multicultural LGBTQ Identities:

Intersectionality recognizes that individuals possess multiple social identities that intersect and interact with each other. For LGBTQ individuals from multicultural backgrounds, their LGBTQ identity intersects with their cultural, ethnic, and religious identities. This intersectionality influences their experiences, perspectives, and challenges, creating unique narratives within the LGBTQ community.

2. Cultural Attitudes and Acceptance:

Cultural attitudes towards LGBTQ individuals vary across different communities and societies. Some cultures may be more accepting and affirming, while others may hold conservative views. Understanding and exploring the diverse cultural attitudes and the progress made towards acceptance within various cultural contexts are important steps toward promoting inclusivity and embracing multicultural LGBTQ experiences.

3. Coming Out and Cultural Expectations:

Coming out as LGBTQ within multicultural contexts can present additional challenges. Family expectations, cultural norms, and religious beliefs may influence the acceptance or rejection LGBTQ individuals face. Navigating these expectations while embracing one's authentic self requires courage and resilience. By discussing the triumphs and challenges of coming out within multicultural contexts, we shed light on the diverse experiences and provide support and understanding.

4. Balancing Multiple Identities:

LGBTQ individuals from multicultural backgrounds often navigate the complexities of balancing multiple identities. They must reconcile their LGBTQ identity with their cultural heritage, traditions, and values. Embracing and honoring diverse aspects of one's identity can be a journey of self-discovery and self-acceptance. By exploring strategies for navigating and celebrating multiple identities, we empower individuals to embrace their authentic selves.

5. LGBTQ Activism in Multicultural Communities:

LGBTQ activism within multicultural communities plays a vital role in promoting acceptance, advocating for rights, and creating safe spaces. This activism takes various forms, such as community organizations, grassroots movements, and advocacy initiatives. By highlighting the diverse LGBTQ activism within multicultural communities, we showcase the resilience and determination of individuals working towards social change.

6. LGBTQ Migration and Experiences:

LGBTQ individuals from multicultural backgrounds may face unique challenges related to migration and seeking asylum. Some may migrate to escape persecution based on their sexual orientation or gender identity. Understanding and addressing the specific challenges faced by LGBTQ migrants, providing support, and advocating for their rights are essential for ensuring their well-being and inclusion.

7. Celebrating Diversity and Cultural Traditions:

LGBTQ individuals from multicultural backgrounds bring a wealth of cultural traditions, celebrations, and customs into LGBTQ spaces. These individuals find ways to integrate their cultural heritage into their LGBTQ identities, creating vibrant and inclusive communities. By highlighting events, pride celebrations, and cultural festivals that celebrate the diversity of multicultural LGBTQ experiences, we promote inclusivity and cultural appreciation.

8. Building Bridges and Fostering Understanding:

Building bridges between LGBTQ communities and multicultural communities is crucial for fostering understanding and promoting acceptance. Through education, dialogue, and cultural exchange, we can bridge the gaps, challenge stereotypes, and foster empathy. By discussing the importance of building bridges and fostering understanding, we encourage mutual respect and appreciation among diverse communities.

As we conclude this part , it is evident that embracing multicultural LGBTQ experiences is essential for creating an inclusive and diverse LGBTQ community. By recognizing and celebrating the intersectionality of LGBTQ identities with cultural, ethnic, and religious backgrounds, we foster understanding, promote acceptance, and celebrate diversity. Let us continue to embrace and learn from the diverse experiences of LGBTQ individuals from multicultural backgrounds, working together to create a future where all LGBTQ individuals feel seen, valued, and included.

Religion, Spirituality, and LGBTQ Identity

In this part , we delve into the intricate relationship between religion, spirituality, and LGBTQ identity. Religion and spirituality often hold profound significance in people's lives, providing them with a sense of purpose, moral guidance, and a connection to something greater. However, for many LGBTQ individuals, their sexual orientation or gender identity can clash with traditional religious teachings, leading to internal conflicts, exclusion, and even discrimination. By exploring the triumphs and trials of navigating the intersection of religion, spirituality, and LGBTQ identity, we aim to foster understanding, promote dialogue, and facilitate reconciliation.

1. Religious Teachings and LGBTQ Acceptance:

Religious traditions have diverse perspectives on LGBTQ acceptance, with some embracing and affirming LGBTQ individuals, while others hold conservative beliefs. It is crucial to explore the teachings, scriptures, and interpretations within different religious contexts that shape the acceptance or rejection of LGBTQ individuals.

2. Internal Conflict and Self-Acceptance:

LGBTQ individuals who hold religious beliefs that conflict with their sexual orientation or gender identity often experience internal conflict. They face the challenge of reconciling their faith with their authentic selves. Understanding their journey of self-acceptance, self-discovery, and finding peace between their faith and LGBTQ identity is essential.

3. Progressive Religious Movements:

Highlighting progressive religious movements that embrace LGBTQ individuals and advocate for LGBTQ rights within religious contexts can inspire hope and demonstrate the possibility of inclusive and affirming religious communities. Sharing stories of religious communities that have evolved and become more accepting creates spaces where LGBTQ individuals can feel safe and supported.

4. Religious Conversion and LGBTQ Identity:

Some LGBTQ individuals may choose to convert to a different religious tradition that aligns more closely with their LGBTQ identity. Examining their experiences, challenges, and triumphs can shed light on the process of finding religious and spiritual communities that fully embrace their authentic selves.

5. Healing Religious Trauma:

The rejection, discrimination, and harmful practices like conversion therapies experienced by LGBTQ individuals within religious contexts can lead to religious trauma. Exploring strategies for healing, seeking support, and reclaiming spirituality in the aftermath of religious trauma is crucial for their well-being and resilience.

6. Intersections of Faith and Activism:

LGBTQ individuals who simultaneously navigate their faith and LGBTQ identities often play significant roles within faith-based activism and social justice movements. Understanding how they reconcile their faith with their activism can inspire others and demonstrate the possibility of harmoniously integrating religious beliefs and LGBTQ advocacy.

7. Interfaith Dialogue and Cooperation:

Fostering interfaith dialogue and cooperation is key to promoting understanding, respect, and inclusivity for LGBTQ individuals across religious communities. Showcasing examples of interfaith initiatives that bridge the gaps between religious traditions and the LGBTQ community can encourage mutual understanding and collaboration.

8. Reconciling Faith and LGBTQ Identity:

Sharing personal stories of individuals who have successfully reconciled their faith and LGBTQ identity can provide guidance and inspiration to those navigating a similar journey. Offering resources, guidance, and support for individuals seeking to reconcile their religious beliefs with their LGBTQ identity is vital for their well-being and sense of belonging.

By ending this sub topic, the intersection of religion, spirituality, and LGBTQ identity is a complex and deeply personal journey for many individuals. By fostering understanding, promoting dialogue, and facilitating reconciliation, we can create spaces where LGBTQ individuals can authentically embrace their faith and LGBTQ identity simultaneously. Through education, advocacy, and compassionate conversations, we can work towards a future where religious and spiritual communities embrace and support LGBTQ individuals, allowing them to fully explore their spirituality while being true to themselves.

Navigating Challenges and Achievements

We explore the intricate intersection of ability and LGBTQ identities, with a specific focus on the challenges and achievements of LGBTQ individuals with disabilities. The LGBTQ community encompasses a diverse range of individuals, including those with varying abilities and disabilities. By delving into the triumphs and trials faced by LGBTQ individuals with disabilities, we aim to promote understanding, raise awareness, and advocate for the rights and well-being of this marginalized group.

1. Understanding Intersectionality:

Intersectionality is a concept that recognizes how various aspects of a person's identity, such as gender, race, sexuality, and ability, intersect and shape their experiences. In this section, we discuss the application of intersectionality to LGBTQ individuals with disabilities, exploring how societal perceptions, ableism, and discrimination can influence their lives.

2. LGBTQ Disabilities and Visibility:

LGBTQ individuals with disabilities often face unique challenges when it comes to visibility within both LGBTQ and disability communities. We delve into the importance of representation and inclusion, highlighting the need to raise awareness and foster acceptance for LGBTQ individuals with disabilities.

3. Accessibility in LGBTQ Spaces:

LGBTQ individuals with disabilities may encounter barriers in accessing and participating in LGBTQ spaces and events. This section explores the challenges they face and emphasizes the significance of creating inclusive and accessible environments that cater to the diverse needs of the LGBTQ community.

4. Health Care Disparities:

LGBTQ individuals with disabilities may experience specific health care disparities, including limited access to quality care and support. We examine the barriers they encounter and discuss the importance of inclusive and culturally competent health care practices that address their unique needs.

5. Intersections of Identity and Self-Acceptance:

Navigating multiple marginalized identities can pose challenges and opportunities for self-acceptance among LGBTQ individuals with disabilities. This section explores their journey of self-discovery, self-acceptance, and finding empowerment within the intersection of their LGBTQ and disability identities.

6. Advocacy and Disability Rights:

Advocacy efforts play a vital role in advancing disability rights within the LGBTQ community. We highlight the achievements and collaborations between disability rights organizations and LGBTQ advocacy groups, emphasizing the importance of collective efforts in fighting for equality and inclusion.

7. Support Networks and Community Building:

Support networks and community building are essential for LGBTQ individuals with disabilities. This section discusses the role of these networks in providing social connections, peer support, and empowerment, as well as the need for creating inclusive spaces that cater to their unique needs.

8. Celebrating Achievements:

We showcase the achievements and contributions of LGBTQ individuals with disabilities across various fields, including activism, arts, academia, and professional spheres. By highlighting their resilience, talents, and successes, we aim to recognize and celebrate the remarkable milestones they have achieved despite the barriers they face.

The experiences of LGBTQ individuals with disabilities are shaped by the intersection of their abilities, identities, and societal perceptions. By understanding their challenges and celebrating their achievements, we can work towards a more inclusive and accessible society that recognizes and values the contributions of LGBTQ individuals with disabilities. Let us strive for equal rights, representation, and support, ensuring that all LGBTQ individuals, regardless of their abilities, can live fulfilling lives and participate fully in all aspects of society.

CHAPTER FIVE

ALLIES AND SUPPORT

The Roles of Allies in LGBTQ Advocacy

In this chapter, we delve into the crucial role that allies play in LGBTQ advocacy. An ally is an individual who supports and advocates for the rights, well-being, and equality of the LGBTQ community, even if they do not personally identify as LGBTQ. By exploring the different roles that allies fulfill, we aim to underscore the significance of allyship in creating inclusive and accepting societies.

1. Understanding Allyship:

Allyship is a concept that involves actively supporting and standing in solidarity with the

LGBTQ community. In this section, we explain the importance of allyship in LGBTQ advocacy and discuss the qualities and characteristics of effective allies, such as empathy, open-mindedness, and a willingness to learn.

2. Education and Awareness:

Allies have a crucial role in educating themselves and others about LGBTQ issues. They work to challenge stereotypes, biases, and misconceptions through continuous learning and awareness-raising initiatives. By becoming knowledgeable about LGBTQ history, terminology, and experiences, allies can better advocate for the rights and well-being of the LGBTQ community.

3. Advocacy and Amplification:

Allies use their privilege, platform, and influence to advocate for LGBTQ rights and amplify the voices of LGBTQ individuals. They speak out against discrimination, support policy changes, and work to create a more inclusive society. Allies understand the importance of using their position to raise awareness and promote positive change.

4. Creating Safe and Inclusive Spaces:

Allies play a significant role in creating safe and inclusive environments for LGBTQ individuals. They actively challenge and address discrimination, harassment, and exclusion in various settings such as schools, workplaces, and communities. Allies work to ensure that LGBTQ individuals feel accepted, respected, and supported in all aspects of their lives.

5. Support and Validation:

Emotional support and validation are crucial for the well-being of LGBTQ individuals. Allies provide a listening ear, offer validation, and help combat feelings of isolation and marginalization. They create a sense of belonging by standing up against prejudice and offering unconditional support to LGBTQ individuals.

6. Collaboration and Partnership:

Allies collaborate and partner with LGBTQ individuals and organizations to advance LGBTQ rights. They recognize that collective efforts are more effective in creating change. By working together, allies and LGBTQ individuals can have a greater impact in promoting equality, fostering understanding, and challenging discriminatory practices.

7. Allyship in Different Spheres:

Allyship is relevant in various contexts, including families, schools, workplaces, and religious institutions. In each sphere, allies face specific challenges and opportunities. They strive to create inclusive and accepting environments by promoting LGBTQ acceptance and challenging homophobia, biphobia, and transphobia.

8. Continual Learning and Growth:

Effective allies engage in continual learning and self-reflection. They stay informed about LGBTQ issues, listen to diverse voices within the community, and adapt their allyship practices to be more inclusive and effective. Allies recognize that they are on a journey of growth and are committed to evolving their understanding and support.

Allies play a crucial role in LGBTQ advocacy by actively supporting and advocating for the rights and well-being of the LGBTQ community. Through education, awareness, advocacy, and creating safe spaces, allies contribute to the fight for equality and acceptance. Their role as allies is essential in fostering inclusive societies that embrace diversity and respect the rights of all individuals, regardless of their sexual orientation or gender identity. Let us celebrate and encourage more individuals to embrace allyship, creating a world where LGBTQ individuals can live with dignity, acceptance, and equality.

Support Networks and Safe Spaces

Support networks and safe spaces are integral components of the LGBTQ community, providing essential support, understanding, and a sense of belonging. In this chapter, we explore the significance of these networks and spaces and their positive impact on the well-being and empowerment of LGBTQ individuals. By examining the benefits, creation, and different types of support networks and safe spaces, we highlight their role in fostering a supportive and inclusive environment.

1. Understanding Support Networks:

Support networks are groups of individuals who come together to provide emotional, social, and practical support to LGBTQ individuals. These networks can be formal or informal and offer a sense of community, understanding, and validation.

2. Benefits of Support Networks:

Support networks offer numerous benefits to LGBTQ individuals. They provide a safe and non-judgmental space for sharing experiences, emotions, and challenges. Support networks can help reduce isolation, enhance self-esteem, and promote personal growth and empowerment.

3. Creating Safe Spaces:

Safe spaces are environments where LGBTQ individuals feel welcomed, accepted, and respected. These spaces aim to provide emotional and physical safety, free from discrimination, prejudice, and harassment. They foster a sense of belonging and allow individuals to express themselves authentically.

4. LGBTQ Support Organizations:

LGBTQ support organizations play a crucial role in providing resources, advocacy, and support services to the community. They offer a wide range of programs, including counseling, helplines, community centers, and educational initiatives. These organizations connect LGBTQ individuals with vital resources and create spaces for empowerment and collective action.

5. Peer Support and Mentoring:

Peer support and mentoring programs within the LGBTQ community provide guidance, validation, and a sense of camaraderie. These programs match individuals with similar experiences, allowing them to share knowledge, advice, and emotional support. Peer support and mentoring foster resilience, personal growth, and a stronger sense of community.

6. Online Communities and Virtual Support:

Online communities and virtual support platforms have become increasingly important in providing support to LGBTQ individuals, particularly for those who may face geographical or social limitations. These spaces offer a sense of connection, information sharing, and access to resources. However, it is important to ensure online safety and prioritize the authenticity and reliability of the platforms.

7. Support Networks for Specific LGBTQ Identities:

Recognizing the diverse experiences within the LGBTQ community, specialized support networks exist for specific identities. These networks address the unique challenges faced by transgender individuals, bisexual individuals, LGBTQ youth, and other specific groups. They provide tailored support, resources, and advocacy to meet their specific needs.

8. Empowerment and Personal Growth:

Support networks and safe spaces empower LGBTQ individuals to embrace their identities, advocate for their rights, and achieve personal growth. By offering a supportive and validating environment, these networks contribute to increased self-acceptance, resilience, and the development of leadership skills.

Support networks and safe spaces are vital components of the LGBTQ community, providing essential support, understanding, and empowerment. By fostering a sense of community, validation, and personal growth, these networks contribute to the overall well-being and resilience of LGBTQ individuals. It is crucial to recognize and support the creation of inclusive support networks and safe spaces that cater to the diverse needs of the community. Through these networks, let us continue to build a more accepting and supportive society where LGBTQ individuals can thrive and live authentically.

Advocacy Organizations And Social Change

Advocacy organizations play a crucial role in driving social change and promoting the rights and well-being of marginalized communities, including the LGBTQ community. These organizations are dedicated to advocating for policy changes, raising awareness, providing support and resources, and challenging discriminatory practices. Their ultimate goal is to create a more inclusive and equitable society.

1. What are Advocacy Organizations?

Advocacy organizations are non-profit entities or grassroots movements that work to influence public opinion, policies, and legislation in favor of a particular cause or community. In the context of LGBTQ advocacy, these organizations focus on advancing LGBTQ rights, fighting discrimination, and promoting acceptance and equality.

2. Goals of Advocacy Organizations:

The primary goals of LGBTQ advocacy organizations include:

- Promoting legal protections: Advocacy organizations work to enact and strengthen laws that protect LGBTQ individuals from discrimination in various areas, such as employment, housing, healthcare, and education.

- Raising awareness: These organizations strive to educate the public about LGBTQ issues, challenges, and the importance of equality. They engage in public campaigns, community outreach, and media initiatives to foster understanding and empathy.

- Challenging stigma and discrimination: Advocacy organizations challenge societal attitudes and biases that contribute to discrimination against LGBTQ individuals. They work to create inclusive environments and combat homophobia, biphobia, and transphobia.

- Providing support and resources: Many advocacy organizations offer support services, counseling, helplines, and resources to LGBTQ individuals and their families. They create safe spaces and networks that foster personal growth, resilience, and empowerment.

3. Strategies of Advocacy Organizations:

Advocacy organizations employ various strategies to bring about social change, including:

- Lobbying and policy advocacy: They engage with lawmakers and government officials to promote LGBTQ-friendly policies and legislation.

- Public education and awareness campaigns: Through media, events, and online platforms, these organizations educate the public, challenge stereotypes, and dispel myths about LGBTQ individuals.

- Community organizing: Advocacy organizations facilitate community engagement, mobilize grassroots efforts, and promote collective action to effect change.

- Legal challenges: They may initiate legal cases to challenge discriminatory laws or practices and set legal precedents that protect LGBTQ rights.

- Coalition building: Advocacy organizations often collaborate with other social justice movements and community organizations to amplify their impact and build alliances for collective action.

4. Impact and Social Change:

Advocacy organizations have made significant strides in achieving social change for the LGBTQ community. Their efforts have contributed to the decriminalization of homosexuality, the legalization of same-sex marriage, the implementation of anti-discrimination laws, and increased visibility and acceptance of LGBTQ individuals in many societies.

By raising awareness, influencing policies, and empowering LGBTQ individuals, advocacy organizations have played a pivotal role in shifting societal attitudes, promoting equality, and creating safer and more inclusive environments. However, their work is ongoing, as there are still challenges to overcome, such as combating systemic discrimination, addressing health disparities, and ensuring full legal protection and rights for all LGBTQ individuals.

Advocacy organizations are at the forefront of driving social change and promoting the rights and well-being of the LGBTQ community. Through their advocacy efforts, they work to challenge discrimination, raise awareness, provide support, and advocate for policy changes. By striving for equality and acceptance, these organizations contribute to creating a more inclusive and equitable society where LGBTQ individuals can live with dignity, respect, and equal rights.

CHAPTER SIX

PROGRESS AND ON GOING CHALLENGES

Historical Milestones in LGBTQ

This chapter explores the historical milestones in LGBTQ rights, tracing the progress made in the fight for equality and acceptance. It delves into key moments, legal victories, and societal changes that have shaped the LGBTQ rights movement. While celebrating the milestones achieved, we also acknowledge the ongoing challenges faced by the LGBTQ community, highlighting the importance of continued activism and advocacy.

1. Pre-Stonewall Era:

- Discuss the historical context of LGBTQ rights prior to the Stonewall uprising in 1969.

- Explore the underground LGBTQ communities, early LGBTQ activism, and the challenges faced by LGBTQ individuals during this period.

2. Stonewall Uprising:

- Detail the events of the Stonewall uprising and its significance as a turning point in the LGBTQ rights movement.

- Discuss the impact of the uprising in mobilizing the community and sparking widespread activism.

3. Legal Milestones:

- Highlight landmark legal victories that have advanced LGBTQ rights, such as the decriminalization of homosexuality, anti-discrimination protections, and the legalization of same-sex marriage.

- Discuss the legal challenges faced by the LGBTQ community and ongoing efforts to secure comprehensive legal protections.

4. HIV/AIDS Crisis:

- Examine the impact of the HIV/AIDS crisis on the LGBTQ community and the subsequent advocacy efforts for healthcare access, research, and destigmatization.

- Discuss the resilience and activism that emerged from this devastating period.

5. Transgender Rights:

- Explore the milestones and challenges in the fight for transgender rights, including legal recognition, healthcare access, and combating discrimination.

- Discuss the ongoing struggles faced by transgender individuals, including violence, healthcare disparities, and legislative battles.

6. Military Service:

- Examine the progress and challenges in the inclusion of LGBTQ individuals in the military, including the repeal of "Don't Ask, Don't Tell" and the ongoing fight for transgender military service.

7. Global LGBTQ Rights:

- Discuss the global landscape of LGBTQ rights, including milestones and ongoing challenges faced by LGBTQ communities in different countries.

- Highlight international advocacy efforts and the importance of global solidarity in advancing LGBTQ rights worldwide.

8. Intersectionality and Inclusion:

- Emphasize the importance of intersectionality within the LGBTQ rights movement, recognizing the diverse experiences and challenges faced by LGBTQ individuals based on race, ethnicity, gender, and socioeconomic factors.

- Discuss efforts to promote inclusivity and intersectional advocacy within the LGBTQ community.

The historical milestones in LGBTQ rights demonstrate the progress made in the fight for equality and acceptance. From the Stonewall uprising to landmark legal victories and global advocacy, significant strides have been achieved. However, ongoing challenges remain, including discrimination, violence, healthcare disparities, and legal obstacles. The chapter highlights the importance of continued activism, allyship, and advocacy to address these challenges and create a more inclusive and equitable society for all LGBTQ individuals. By understanding the historical context and ongoing struggles, we can inspire future generations to continue the fight for full equality and celebrate the progress that has been made thus far.

Continuing Battles for Equality

Despite significant progress in LGBTQ rights, the struggle for full equality and acceptance is an ongoing battle. This chapter explores the persistent challenges faced by the LGBTQ community, highlighting the areas where further advancements are needed. By examining these ongoing battles, we can deepen our understanding of the work that lies ahead and inspire continued efforts to create a more inclusive and equitable society.

1. Workplace Discrimination:

- Discuss the continued presence of workplace discrimination against LGBTQ individuals, including unequal treatment, harassment, and barriers to career advancement.

- Highlight the need for comprehensive anti-discrimination laws and policies that protect LGBTQ employees in all sectors.

2. Healthcare Disparities:

- Address the healthcare disparities faced by the LGBTQ community, such as limited access to LGBTQ-inclusive care, higher rates of mental health issues, and transgender-specific healthcare challenges.

- Advocate for improved access to competent and inclusive healthcare services, increased LGBTQ cultural competency training for healthcare professionals, and policy reforms that address these disparities.

3. Homelessness and Housing Insecurity:

- Explore the issue of LGBTQ homelessness and housing insecurity, often resulting from family rejection, discrimination, and lack of affordable and LGBTQ-inclusive housing options.

- Advocate for increased funding and support for LGBTQ-specific shelters, affordable housing initiatives, and comprehensive programs addressing the unique needs of LGBTQ individuals experiencing homelessness.

4. Youth Bullying and Suicide Prevention:

- Discuss the persistent problem of bullying and harassment faced by LGBTQ youth, which contributes to higher rates of mental health issues and suicide.

- Advocate for comprehensive anti-bullying policies in schools, inclusive LGBTQ education, and the implementation of supportive resources and programs to prevent bullying and promote mental well-being.

5. Transgender Rights and Advocacy:

- Focus on the ongoing struggles for transgender rights, including legal recognition, access to affirming healthcare, protection from discrimination, and the unique challenges faced by transgender youth.

- Advocate for transgender-inclusive policies, improved legal protections, increased awareness about transgender issues, and support for transgender individuals in all areas of life.

6. Intersectionality and Racial Justice:

- Highlight the importance of addressing intersectional struggles faced by LGBTQ individuals of different races and ethnicities, recognizing the compounding effects of racism, homophobia, and transphobia.

- Advocate for inclusive and intersectional approaches to LGBTQ advocacy, prioritizing racial justice, and amplifying the voices of marginalized LGBTQ communities.

7. Conversion Therapy:

- Address the harmful and discredited practice of conversion therapy, which aims to change a person's sexual orientation or gender identity.

- Advocate for comprehensive bans on conversion therapy, increased awareness about its dangers, and support for survivors through accessible mental health resources and counseling services.

8. Immigration and Asylum:

- Discuss the challenges faced by LGBTQ individuals within the immigration system, including persecution, discrimination, and limited access to asylum.

- Advocate for inclusive immigration policies that consider LGBTQ-specific factors, provide protections for LGBTQ asylum seekers, and ensure fair treatment within the immigration process.

The fight for LGBTQ equality continues in various domains, requiring ongoing advocacy, education, and support. By acknowledging the ongoing battles faced by the LGBTQ community, we can work towards a future where all individuals are free from discrimination, have equal rights and opportunities, and can live authentically. It is through collective efforts and unwavering commitment that we can overcome these challenges and create a society that embraces and celebrates the diversity of the LGBTQ community.

Education and Awareness for a More Inclusive Society

Here, we explore the importance of education and awareness in creating a more inclusive society for the LGBTQ community. By examining the role of education, promoting LGBTQ-inclusive curricula, and raising awareness about LGBTQ issues, we aim to highlight the transformative power of knowledge in fostering acceptance, understanding, and equality.

1. The Power of Education:

Education plays a pivotal role in challenging stereotypes, combating discrimination, and promoting inclusivity. We discuss the significance of inclusive education that incorporates LGBTQ perspectives, histories, and experiences.

2. LGBTQ-Inclusive Curricula:

We examine the importance of developing and implementing LGBTQ-inclusive curricula in schools and educational institutions. This section explores the benefits of teaching about diverse sexual orientations, gender identities, and LGBTQ history, highlighting the positive impact on students' understanding and acceptance.

3. Educating Teachers and Staff:

To create LGBTQ-inclusive learning environments, it is essential to provide comprehensive education and training to teachers and educational staff. We discuss the importance of professional development programs that equip educators with the knowledge and skills to support LGBTQ students and create inclusive spaces.

4. Promoting Acceptance and Tolerance:

Education and awareness initiatives can foster acceptance and tolerance among students, teachers, and the broader community. We explore strategies such as workshops, guest speakers, and awareness campaigns that promote empathy, respect, and understanding for LGBTQ individuals.

5. Addressing Bullying and Harassment:

LGBTQ students are more susceptible to bullying and harassment. This section focuses on the importance of implementing anti-bullying policies, promoting safe spaces, and providing resources to address bullying incidents effectively. It also emphasizes the need for ongoing support for LGBTQ students.

6. LGBTQ Resource Centers:

We discuss the role of LGBTQ resource centers in educational institutions and communities. These centers provide valuable resources, support networks, and educational programs to promote inclusivity, support LGBTQ students, and raise awareness about LGBTQ issues.

7. Parent and Community Engagement:

Education and awareness efforts extend beyond the classroom. This section explores the importance of engaging parents, families, and the broader community in understanding and supporting LGBTQ individuals. We discuss strategies for fostering dialogue, providing resources, and promoting acceptance at home and in the community.

8. Collaborating with LGBTQ Organizations:

Collaborating with LGBTQ organizations can enhance educational efforts and promote inclusivity. We highlight the benefits of partnerships between educational institutions and LGBTQ organizations to develop educational resources, provide guest speakers, and offer support to LGBTQ students and their allies.

9. Continuing Education and Lifelong Learning:

Education and awareness are ongoing processes. This section emphasizes the importance of continued education and lifelong learning for educators, students, and community members. It explores opportunities for professional development, staying informed about LGBTQ issues, and challenging biases and misconceptions.

Education and awareness are essential tools for creating a more inclusive society for the LGBTQ community. By incorporating LGBTQ-inclusive curricula, providing training for educators, addressing bullying, engaging parents and the community, and collaborating with LGBTQ organizations, we can promote acceptance, understanding, and equality. Let us continue to prioritize education and awareness efforts to build a society where all individuals are respected, celebrated, and included, regardless of their sexual orientation or gender identity.

CONCLUSION

JOURNEYING FORWARD WITH RESILIENCE AND HOPE

In this chapter, we explore the concept of journeying forward with resilience and hope in the context of the LGBTQ community. We delve into the experiences, challenges, and triumphs that LGBTQ individuals face on their personal journeys, emphasizing the importance of resilience and maintaining a positive outlook for a better future.

1. Understanding Resilience:

Resilience refers to the ability to adapt, bounce back, and thrive in the face of adversity. We discuss how resilience plays a crucial role in the lives of LGBTQ individuals, enabling them to navigate societal challenges, discrimination, and personal setbacks.

2. Embracing Personal Growth:

Personal growth is a transformative process that occurs as individuals embrace their identities and navigate their unique journeys. We explore how LGBTQ individuals can harness their experiences, learn from them, and use them as catalysts for personal growth, self-acceptance, and empowerment.

3. Cultivating Self-Care:

Self-care is essential for maintaining emotional well-being and resilience. We discuss the importance of self-care practices, such as self-reflection, self-compassion, and seeking support, to nurture resilience and maintain a positive mindset throughout the journey.

4. Finding Strength in Community:

The LGBTQ community provides a valuable support system and a sense of belonging. We explore how connecting with supportive communities, engaging in LGBTQ organizations, and participating in advocacy efforts can strengthen resilience and inspire hope for a more inclusive future.

5. Celebrating Success and Milestones:

Recognizing and celebrating personal achievements and milestones is vital for building resilience and fostering a positive outlook. We discuss the significance of acknowledging progress, overcoming challenges, and celebrating the accomplishments of LGBTQ individuals on their journeys.

6. Navigating Setbacks and Challenges:

Setbacks and challenges are inevitable on any journey. We explore strategies for navigating setbacks, such as resilience-building techniques, seeking support, and reframing obstacles as opportunities for growth. We emphasize the importance of resilience in bouncing back and moving forward.

7. Inspiring Hope for the Future:

Hope serves as a guiding force for LGBTQ individuals as they journey forward. We discuss the power of hope in inspiring resilience, fostering a sense of purpose, and driving positive change. We highlight examples of progress, acceptance, and LGBTQ rights advancements to inspire hope for a more inclusive future.

8. Creating a Supportive Environment:

Building a supportive environment is crucial for LGBTQ individuals on their journeys. We explore the role of allies, educational institutions, workplaces, and society at large in creating inclusive and accepting spaces. We discuss the importance of fostering environments that nurture resilience, hope, and the well-being of LGBTQ individuals.

Conclusion:

Journeying forward with resilience and hope is a transformative process for LGBTQ individuals. By embracing personal growth, practicing self-care, finding strength in community, celebrating successes, navigating challenges, and inspiring hope for the future, LGBTQ individuals can thrive and create positive change. Let us continue to support and uplift one another, fostering resilience, hope, and a brighter future for all members of the LGBTQ community.